THIS WALKER BOOK BELONGS TO:

The author wishes to thank the following
for their help and co-operation:
MERCEDES-BENZ • KING TRAILERS •
HOYNOR • ABBEY HILL • BOEING •
TEREX • PORT OF TILBURY • SCHMIDT •
CRANE FRUEHAUF • GENERAL MOTORS •
DENNIS EAGLE • VOLVO BM •
LONDON FIRE SERVICE

First published 1991 by
Walker Books Ltd
87 Vauxhall Walk, London SE11 5HJ

This edition published 1992
Reprinted 1993

Printed and bound in Hong Kong by
Sheck Wah Tong Printing Press Ltd

British Library Cataloguing in Publication Data
A catalogue record for this book is
available from the British Library.
ISBN 0-7445-2095-9

DEREK RADFORD
TRANSPORT MACHINES
AND WHAT THEY DO

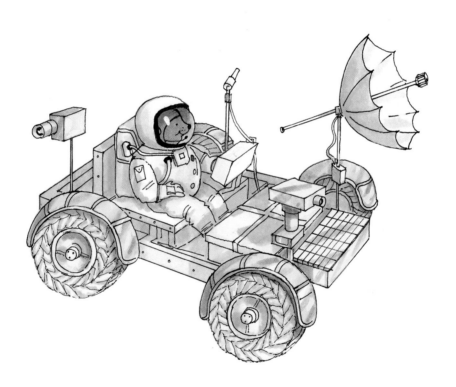

WALKER BOOKS

LONDON

Cargo plane

Some aeroplanes carry passengers. Other planes carry only cargo. The cargo, which might be machinery, motors, food or clothing, is packed in steel containers.

Inside the aircraft, the heavy containers move on rollers.

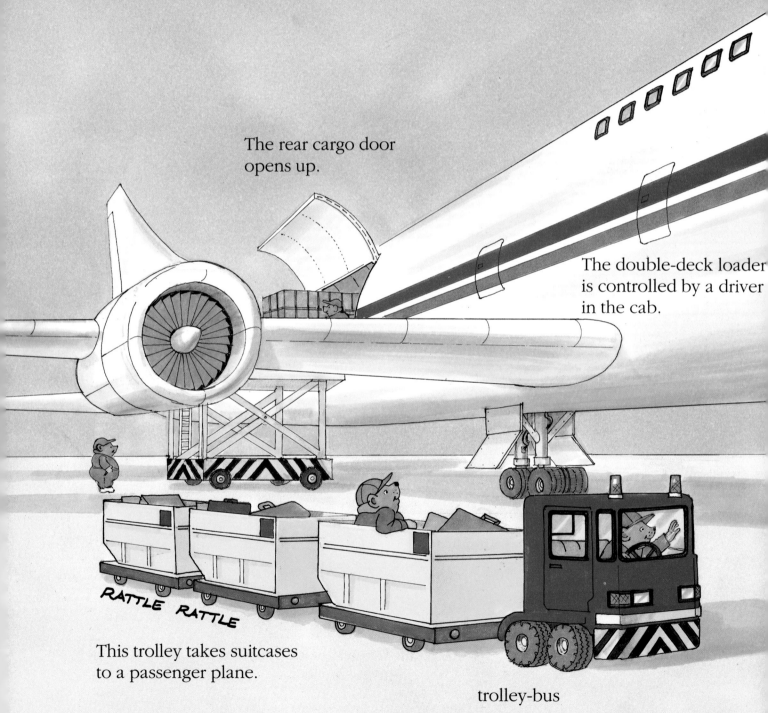

The rear cargo door opens up.

The double-deck loader is controlled by a driver in the cab.

RATTLE RATTLE

This trolley takes suitcases to a passenger plane.

trolley-bus

nose cone

The nose cone of the
aeroplane lifts up.

A double-deck loader lifts
the cargo containers up to
the loading deck.

double-deck loader

Hydraulic arms raise
and lower the double-
deck loader.

Logger

Loggers load big tree trunks on to lorries to be taken to the sawmills. Trees take a long time to grow, so new forests must be planted to replace the ones cut down.

WB/1810

Forests are specially planted for timber and paper-making.

The driver opens and closes the jaws to pick up and stack logs.

BRRR!

It's cold work in the north.

This diesel lorry can carry 24 tonnes.

logger

The giant logger has strong mechanical jaws for lifting and carrying heavy trunks. It can lift 26 tonnes at once.

WB/1811

WB/1812

These logs have been felled by chainsaws.

Sea cargo

Most sea cargo – cars, food, machinery and so on – travels in steel containers. Some containers are chilled.

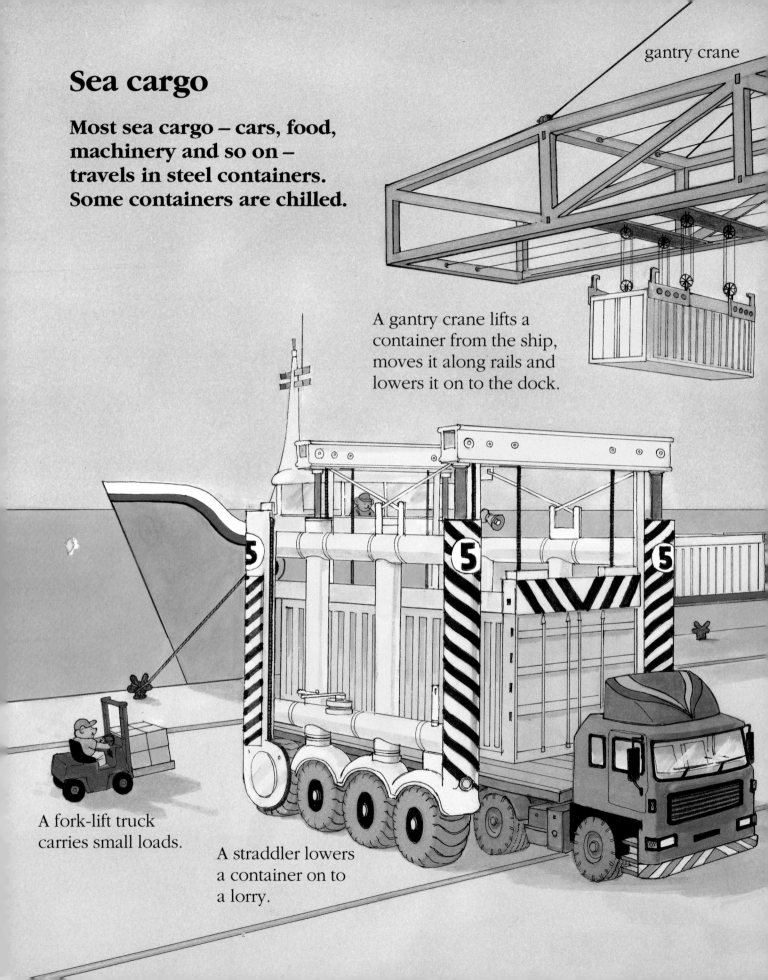

gantry crane

A gantry crane lifts a container from the ship, moves it along rails and lowers it on to the dock.

A fork-lift truck carries small loads.

A straddler lowers a container on to a lorry.

A driver controls the gantry crane from this cabin.

A straddler carrier goes to pick up a container.

container

The gantry crane moves along a track.

straddler carrier

A lorry waits for a straddler to bring a container.

Petrol tanker

Petrol is transported to garages in sealed tankers. A tanker has seven separate compartments so that it can carry different grades of petrol.

The garage owner uses a long dip-stick to check the amount of petrol delivered.

As well as rear tail-lights, the tanker has rear head-lights for backing up in the dark.

Hoses are stored round the tank. They can be locked together to make an extra-long hose.

CLANG!

LAMMABLE LIQUID

GARAGE

Each compartment has its
own discharge valve.

The garage's underground
supply tanks are usually well
away from the petrol pumps.

petrol pump

This car has
broken down.

Dump trucks

Giant dump trucks can move huge amounts of earth, stone or sand over bumpy ground.

Controls in the cabin enable the driver to tip the load in the right place.

A safety mesh protects the driver from falling rock.

hydraulic arms

The dump truck can ride over rough ground because each wheel moves independently.

Extending wing mirrors help
the driver to see when he is
backing up and tipping.

wing mirror

Big, deep-tread tyres cope with
mud, sand or jagged rocks.

These dump trucks can
carry up to 35 tonnes.

RUMBLE! RUMBLE!

CRUNCH!!

Car transporter

New vehicles are taken on
special transporters from the
factories where they are built
to the showrooms and garages
where they will be sold.

Each car is fixed with
straps. Cars at the back
have their rear wheels
fitted into chocks.

Loading and unloading must
be done very carefully to
avoid damaging the cars.

A ramp is extended for
loading. Later, it slides
back into the transporter.

Safety bars hold
cars in place.

To make the best use
of space, some cars rest
at an angle.

Levers raise and
lower the car decks.

The load is checked. Cars
for the first delivery must
be positioned so that they
are easy to drive off.

Trucks and trailers

When the circus is on the move, everything is transported in giant trailers towed by powerful trucks. "Everything" includes the big top, the giant wheel, the big dipper, bumper cars and side-shows!

big top

The trailer has support legs so that it can stand alone if the truck is needed elsewhere.

Smoke from the diesel
engine comes out at the
top of the exhaust stack.

aerial

Klaxon horns alert other
motorists on the road.

A CB radio helps drivers
keep in touch on long
journeys.

tool kit

The driver does a repair
to the exhaust stack.

The truck has 10 wheels.
The trailer has 12 wheels.

Snow vehicles

All transport is brought to a halt when snow blocks roads but snow cutters and blowers can clear roads in a matter of hours.

Flashing lights warn other vehicles that the snow machines are at work.

The funnels can blow snow up to 50 metres away.

The cutter breaks up packed snow and forces it out through funnels.

A snow cutter has big scoops at the front.

snow cutter

Steel chains on the cutter's wheels give them better grip.

This vehicle scatters grit on the road to make it less slippery.

WHOOSH!

The driver can move the funnels to send snow in any direction.

snow blower

A snow blower opens its gates and takes loose snow in through funnels.

Low loader

A low loader is a huge carrier used for transporting heavy or slow machines such as excavators, or equipment like boilers and furnaces.

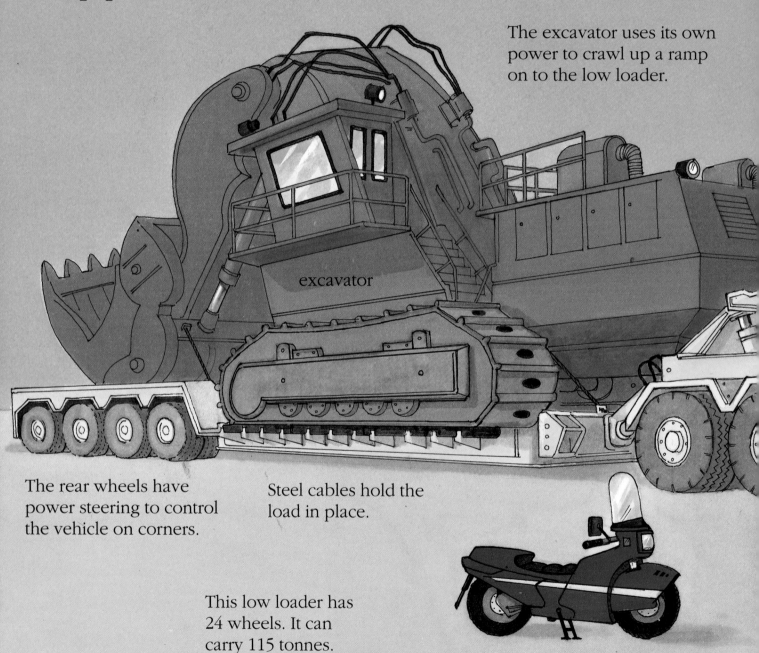

The excavator uses its own power to crawl up a ramp on to the low loader.

excavator

The rear wheels have power steering to control the vehicle on corners.

Steel cables hold the load in place.

This low loader has 24 wheels. It can carry 115 tonnes.

The lorry is articulated, which means it is joined to the low loader but can move freely from side to side.

warning lights

The low loader's route needs to be carefully planned to avoid busy or narrow roads, low bridges and tunnels.

Police outriders make sure that roads are clear

Dustcart

Each day millions of used bottles, cans, boxes and paper are collected by dustcarts and taken to refuse sites or to recycling plants. Today we recycle paper, cans and bottles for re-use.

A sweeper plate inside the dustcart keeps pushing in the rubbish.

SWISH!

SWISH!

sweeper plate

A street cleaner brushes and sucks up dirt.

Plastic bags and rubbish from dustbins are thrown into the dustcart.

Workers wear thick overalls and gloves for protection against dirt and cuts.

Inside the dustcart, the rubbish is packed down under pressure so that it takes up a smaller space.

The steel body of the dustcart has raised ribs to give it extra strength.

DANGER
STAND
CLEAR

At the recycling plant, an ejector plate inside the dustcart pushes the rubbish out.

Space vehicles

Space craft such as Apollo 15 can travel at 40,000km per hour. They are powerful enough to carry astronauts and their equipment to the moon – 380,500km from the earth.

The Space Module orbited the moon while the astronauts worked on the surface.

Batteries provided power.
Top speed: 16 kmph

The Lunar Rover could be located by signals sent out by its navigation equipmen

The Lunar Rover was made of light-weight metals. It weighed 208 kg on earth but only 36 kg on the moon.

Steel wire-mesh wheels grip the surface.

Apollo 15

Lunar Module

The Lunar Module stood on four round feet so that its power thrusters were kept clear of the moon's surface.

The Lunar Rover collected samples of soil and rock.

crater

Fire engine

When the alarm rings at the fire station, all the crew jump on to their engines. One engine carries water and chemical foam. The other engine carries a long, movable ladder.

The extending ladder reaches to the upstairs windows.

Police keep back the crowds.

NEE-NA- NEE -NA!.

Extra water comes from a pipe under the road.

The Fire Chief uses a loud hailer to give instructions.

WHOOSH!

A powerful jet of water is directed at the flames.

Smoke is deadly, so firemen wear oxygen masks.

An axe is used to break down doors.

OXYGEN

MORE WALKER PAPERBACKS
For You to Enjoy

BUILDING MACHINES
by Derek Radford

Another lively title about machines and what they do. In this book you'll find crushers and cranes, hoppers and hammers, dump trucks and drop balls – and lots more.

0-7445-2090-8   £3.99

MACHINES AT WORK
by Gaynor Chapman

Two colourful and absorbing studies of machines at work, on the road and the building site. There are drills and water-pumps, excavators and backhoe loaders, concrete mixers, mobile cranes and many more.

Road Works   0-7445-0916-5
Building Works   0-7445-0917-3
£2.99 each

THE DUMP TRUCK
by Arlene Blanchard and Tony Wells

To and fro, all day long, the sturdy truck fetches and carries loads of rocks and stones across the quarry.

0-7445-3119-5   £3.99

THE TUGBOAT
by Arlene Blanchard and Tony Wells

Tugboat Mary's day is full of activity, towing and pushing big ships – and then she has to answer a distress call.

0-7445-3118-7   £3.99

**Walker Paperbacks are available from most booksellers, or by post from
Walker Books Ltd, PO Box 11, Falmouth, Cornwall TR10 9EN.**

To order, send: Title, author, ISBN number and price for each book ordered, your full name and address,
cheque or postal order for the total amount, plus postage and packing:

UK and BFPO Customers – £1.00 for first book, plus 50p for the second book and plus 30p for each additional book to a maximum charge of £3.00.
Overseas and Eire Customers – £2.00 for first book, plus £1.00 for the second book and plus 50p per copy for each additional book.
Prices are correct at time of going to press, but are subject to change without notice.